M000205469

Letter to the Amazon

UDP | EEPS #41

Letter to the Amazon by Marina Tsvetaeva
First published in French as *Mon Frère féminin* (Mercure de France, 1979)
English Translation © 2016, 2020 A'Dora Phillips & Gaëlle Cogan
Introduction © 2016, 2020 Catherine Ciepiela

Eastern European Poets Series #41
ISBN 978-1-937027-69-8

First Edition, 2016
Second Printing, 2020

Ugly Duckling Presse
The Old American Can Factory
232 Third Street #E-303
Brooklyn, New York 11215

Design by Katherine Bogden
Typeset in Garamond
Printed & bound by McNaughton & Gunn in Saline, Michigan
Covers printed by Prestige Printing, Brooklyn, New York

Distributed to the trade in the USA by Small Press Distribution,
in Canada by Coach House Books via Publishers Group Canada,
and in the United Kingdom by Inpress.

The publication of this book is supported in part by an award from
the National Endowment for the Arts and the continued support of
the New York State Council on the Arts.

Letter to the Amazon

Marina Tsvetaeva

Translated from the French by
A'Dora Phillips & Gaëlle Cogan

Introduction by Catherine Ciepiela

Introduction

From our twenty-first century vantage, we can fully appreciate the modernists' first assaults on conventional artistic and personal expression, made under the pressure of history and from sheer passion for experience. Modernism was a culture-crossing adventure of the spirit that writers of many backgrounds signed up for, among them Marina Tsvetaeva, the Russian poet who authored the French essay here translated into English. She wrote "Letter to the Amazon" ("Lettre à l'Amazone") between 1932 and 1934 while living in Paris, where writers of the city's many diasporas mingled, making it the international capitol of modernism. Her "Letter" was addressed to Natalie Barney, the American lesbian poet who moved to France at the turn of the century to enjoy its freer moral atmosphere. A lost modernist classic, Tsvetaeva's essay plays out a conversation between a Russian émigrée and an American expatriate, both escaped to Paris from their native countries and communicating in French, debating one of modernism's urgent concerns: woman's sexuality as expressed through lesbianism.

Natalie Barney was the earliest and least anguished of the openly lesbian writers of the twentieth century, though she remains almost unknown to American readers because she chose to write in French. In her own time she was an inspiring figure for women writers who claimed their lesbianism; Radclyffe Hall's 1928 novel *The Well of Loneliness*, for instance, featured a character based upon her. Barney's first book was a volume of "portrait-sonnets of women" (*Quelques portrait-sonnets de femmes,* 1900), which her artist mother, Alice Pike Barney, illustrated. In her poetry she celebrated her radical sexuality using strict nineteenth-century forms, in contrast to the free-wheeling, aphoristic prose works for which she is best known. In these writings she is direct, confident, and even gleeful in embracing lesbianism against social norms and authorities. Some of that confidence came to her as the daughter of a very wealthy American industrialist, from whose sway and on whose money she escaped to Paris, where she set herself up as an influential *salonnière,* hosting figures like Paul Valéry and André Gide. Barney's salon—in contrast to the salon of her fellow American lesbian expatriate, Gertrude Stein—was a gathering-place for homosexuals and the center of a lesbian community. (She had earlier tried to establish a neo-Sapphic colony on the island of Lesbos.) Barney ran her own press for women writers and offered them material support, and this was how she came to meet Marina Tsvetaeva.

Tsvetaeva arrived in Paris in 1925 not as an expatriate but as a refugee. Born sixteen years later than Barney, in 1892, she also was a child of privilege in her native Moscow, where her father founded the first Russian museum of classical antiquities, now known as the Pushkin Museum. Both of her parents died prematurely, leaving her a substantial legacy, on which she lived a bohemian life with her husband Sergei Efron and young daughter. During 1914-16 she had a profound affair with Sofia Parnok, known as the Russian Sappho for her frankly lesbian poems; Tsvetaeva wrote an equally frank cycle of poems about their affair, "The Girlfriend" ("Podruga"). She also was writing new poems in which she found her voice as a poet of transgressive attitudes and aesthetics. The Bolshevik revolution that soon followed completely altered her life: she was dispossessed of her fortune and her husband, who left Moscow to fight with the White Army. After their defeat and exile, she emigrated with her daughter to join Efron, living first in Berlin, then in Prague and finally in Paris, the center of the Russian emigration. When she arrived there in 1925, Tsvetaeva was welcomed as a literary celebrity by her fellow émigrés; the half-dozen books of lyrics and long poems she published upon emigrating had established her as one of the most brilliant poets writing in Russian. She soon alienated her émigré audience, though, with her broadminded interest in literary developments back in Soviet Russia. She saw herself as writing within a large European literary context, especially after her intense correspondence (in German) with Rilke in 1926, who wrote his final elegy to her ("O die Verluste ins All, Marina, die stürzenden Sterne!"). Inspired by his example—he wrote a book of poems in French at the end of his career—she began to self-translate some of her poetry and prose into French. Her ambition to enter the world of French letters is what brought her to Natalie Barney's salon. Tsvetaeva may have hoped Barney would aid her financially, as well. Her family, which now included a young son, lived on what she made as a professional writer: a stipend from the Czech government (which was supporting the Russian intelligentsia in exile for political reasons), the modest fees she got for publishing in émigré journals, and the personal generosity of admirers. Efron earned little at casual jobs, once working as a walk-on in the film industry, a not uncommon situation for Russian émigrés, who were barred from the professions in France.

Tsvetaeva visited Barney's salon several times in the early '30s. In a letter to a friend, she described a run-in with Isadora Duncan's brother Raymond in the salon of "an American woman writer." In another letter, she complained that "Nathalie Clifford-Barney" had lost the manuscripts she gave her—namely, her translation into French of one of her long poems, "The Swain" ("Le Gars," 1932), and a French prose piece, "Nine Letters" ("Neuf lettres," 1932), based on her love letters to a fellow Russian émigré. Her hopes for publishing "The Swain" were high, and with good reason. In the late '20s she became friendly with the artist Natalya Goncharova, who emigrated to France from Moscow, where she had led the "primitivist" wing of the Russian avant-garde. Goncharova was famous in Paris and beyond for the vivid stylizations of Russian folk art she brought to her set and costume designs for the Ballets Russes and other companies. Tsvetaeva's "The Swain" ("Molodets," 1921), based on a Russian fairytale about a vampire lover, was crafted in a similar spirit: she wrote the poem in her own modern folkish Russian, rather as Yeats invented his own Gaelic idiom. Goncharova made a set of illustrations for the poem, prompting Tsvetaeva to translate it and seek a French publisher for this remarkable collaboration between two Russian women geniuses. She did not succeed: the poem's innovative prosody seemed to French publishers, in her words, "*too* new, unfamiliar, outside any tradition, not even surrealism." When Barney invited Tsvetaeva to read "The Swain" at her salon, the guests "heard it out in dead silence," according to a friend who accompanied Tsvetaeva. In truth, Tsvetaeva's high modernist writing could not have been more alien to Barney's nineteenth-century poetics, which may be why nothing came of her plans for "The Swain." Barney did, though, offer Tsvetaeva financial help, later joining a committee organized to raise money in her support.

Barney also engaged with Tsvetaeva as a "feminine brother" (Barney's phrase) who cared deeply about lesbian love. In late 1932, Tsvetaeva received from a friend a copy of her *Pensées d'une Amazone* (1918), which Tsvetaeva immediately read and responded to with her "Lettre à l'Amazone." It is not clear whether she sent her "Letter" to Barney, nor whether she ever intended to publish it. (A later version from her notebooks eventually appeared in 1979 under the title *Mon Frère féminin*.) Tsvetaeva's portrait of the lesbian couple was drawn from her affair with Sophia Parnok, right down to the color of the lovers' hair. She tells of a sexually experienced older woman who seduces a younger one, as Parnok seduced Tsvetaeva when she was twenty-four. Parnok was her first and possibly only woman lover, but the experience freed up her sexual attitudes. Just a few years later, snared in multiple erotic entanglements in Moscow's theater world, she declared, "[t]o love only women (for a woman) or only men (for a man), deliberately excluding the standard opposite sex—how awful! But to love only women (for a man) or only men (for a woman), deliberately excluding the non-standard same sex—how boring!" Tsvetaeva, though, tended to portray the male lover as one who harms the loved woman, as she does in her "Letter," easily owning Barney's notion of men as "the enemy." She elevates lesbian love above the heterosexual romance as an encounter of souls—for Tsvetaeva, the highest sort of erotic experience.

Yet this perfect love between women, Tsvetaeva says, founders on a single obstacle: the impossibility of having children. She describes the tragedy of the younger's desire for a child, and the older's pained knowledge that she cannot satisfy her. In her telling, the younger woman inevitably leaves the older, as Tsvetaeva left Parnok to return to Efron, with whom she soon bore a second daughter.

Some readers may see this matter of the child as an obstacle of her own making: Can one not adopt a child? Or bring a child from a previous liaison into a lesbian relationship, as Tsvetaeva brought her own daughter along on trips with Parnok? For Tsvetaeva, these were no substitutes for bearing a child by the beloved. The problem, then, is nature, which is to say, biology. As far as Tsvetaeva was concerned, there was nothing unnatural about lesbian sexuality. But nature enjoins procreation, presenting the lesbian couple with an excruciating contradiction. When she speaks about renunciation at the beginning of her "Letter," she is not speaking, as Barney was in her *Pensées*, about renouncing her sexual instincts but about renouncing her lesbian lover in favor of the child. Tsvetaeva's genuine need for children and family is readable everywhere in her writing, and most readable in her "Letter" when she envisions aging lesbians as living in blank isolation.

Tsvetaeva's elevation of childbearing over erotic fulfillment conflicted not only with Barney's views but with the views of her generation of sexual revolutionaries, who considered procreation a lesser, even opposed, commitment. But her passionately stated case may now feel sympathetic to gay and lesbian couples who are fighting all over the world for the legal right to bear children and build families together. In this way, Tsvetaeva was a century ahead of her time in thinking about human sexual and emotional freedom. She may have welcomed the advances in medical science that make it possible for lesbian couples to bear children with at least one partner's biological stake— advances that have made nature "unnatural," in the way that homosexuality is, in Barney's phrase, "naturally unnatural." What Tsvetaeva certainly achieved in her "Letter" was to think through, with pathos and rigor, an instance in human experience when sexuality and biology create a conflict that individual choice alone can resolve.

Catherine Ciepiela
Amherst, 2016

Letter to the Amazon

I read your book. I feel close to you, as to all women who write. Don't take offense at being one among my "all"—not all women write, only those who are exceptional.

And so, I am close to you, as to any rare person, especially any rare person who is a woman.

I have been thinking of you since the day I saw you—has it been a month? When I was young, I was eager to explain myself to others, I was afraid of missing the wave rising from within to carry me toward the other, I was always afraid of loving no more, of knowing no more. But I am no longer young, and have learned to let almost everything pass—irrevocably.

To have everything to say—and to keep your lips clenched. Everything give—and to not extend your hand. This is the renouncement that you call bourgeois virtue and that, bourgeois or not, virtue or not, is what largely motivates my actions. Renouncement—a motivation? Yes, because controlling a force requires an infinitely more bitter effort than unleashing it—which requires no effort at all. In this sense all natural activity is passive, while all willed passivity is active (effusion—endurance, repression—action). Which is more difficult: to hold a horse back or to let it run? And, given that we are the horse held back—which is harder: to be restrained or to allow our strength free rein? To breathe or not? Do you remember the children's game where all of the honor went to the one who remained in the chest the longest, *suffocating*? A cruel game, and hardly bourgeois.

To act? To let go. Each time I give up, I feel a tremor within. It is me—the earth that quakes. Renouncement? Struggle petrified.

My renouncement also means that I do not deign—to fight with the existing order over anything. The existing order in our case? To read your book, to thank you for it with empty words, to see you again from time to time, "smiling that one may not see you smile"—to pretend that you hadn't written anything and I'd not read anything: as if nothing had passed between us.

I could have done that, can still do it, but for once—I do not want to.

Listen to me, you do not need to respond, you need only to hear. It is a blow I strike straight to your heart, straight to the heart of your cause, your belief, your body, your heart.

A gap in your book, the only one, immense—conscious or not? I don't believe in the unconsciousness of thinking people, still less—in the unconsciousness of thinking people who write, not at all—in the unconsciousness of writers who are women.

This gap, this omission, this black hole—it is the child.

You keep coming back to him. You mention him often yet never discuss him with the depth he deserves. You scatter him here and there, then there again, to avoid granting him the lone cry that you owe him.

This cry, have you never, at the very least—heard it? "If only I could have a child of yours!"

And this jealousy, fierce and unequalled, implacable because it is incurable, incomparable to the other one, the "normal" one, incomparable even to maternal jealousy. This jealousy, pre-science of the inevitable estrangement, these eyes wide open to the child that she will want one day and that you, the oldest, will not be able to give to her. These eyes riveted upon the child to come.

"Lovers do not have children."

Yes, but they die. All of them. Romeo and Juliet; Tristan and Iseult; the Amazon and Achilles; Siegfried and Brunhilde (these potential lovers, these divided united, whose disunion in love prevails over the most complete union). And others. And yet others. Whatever the song, whatever the time, whatever the place. They have no time for the future that the child is, they have no child because they have no future, they have only the present that is their love and death, always present. They die—or their love dies (degenerates into friendship or maternity: old Baucis and Philemon, aging Pulkheria with her venerable son Afanasy—couples as monstrous as they are touching).

Love in itself is childhood. Lovers are children. Children do not have children.

Or—as with Daphnis and Chloe—we know

nothing more of them: even if they survive—
they die, in us, for us.

One cannot *live* off love. The one thing that
survives love is the child.

¶

And this other cry, then, have you not heard
that one either? How I wish for a child—without a man! The tender sigh of a girl, the candid
sigh of an old maid, and even, sometimes, the
desperate sigh of a woman: "How I wish for
one—only *mine*!"

And so it is that the young smiling girl, who
does not want any stranger in her body, who
wants nothing to do with him and what is his,
who wants only what is *mine*, meets at the turn
of a road another *me*, a *she*, whom she need not
fear, against whom she need not defend herself,
for the other cannot hurt her, since one cannot
(at least when young) hurt oneself. A most il-
lusory certitude, one which will waver at the
first distrustful glance of the lover and collapse
under the great heart pangs of her hate.

But let us not get ahead of ourselves: for the
moment she is happy and free, free to love with

the heart, not the body, to love without fear, to love without doing harm.

And when the harm has been done—she discovers that it isn't a harm, after all. Harm—would be: the shame, the regret, the remorse, the disgust. Harm would be to betray her heart with a man, her childhood with the enemy. But here there is no enemy, since it is still *me*, always *me*, a new me, one who had slept in my depths and was roused by this other me, there, in front of me, outside of me, and, at last, *one who can be loved*. She did not have to deny herself to become a woman, she had only to let herself go (to the innermost depths of herself)—had only to let herself be. No crack, no break, no wither.

It comes down to these words:

"O me! O darling *me*."

Oh! It is never out of shame or disgust that she leaves her. It is out of and for another reason altogether.

§

At first, it seems almost as if we are joking.

"What a beautiful baby!"
"Would you like one?"
"Yes. No. Of you—yes."
"But..."
"But it's just a joke."

Another time it is a sigh.
"How I would like..."
"What?"
"Nothing."
"Yes, yes, I know..."
"If you know. But only if—of you."
Silence.

"You're still thinking of that?"
"If you say so."
"You're the one who said so."

She lacks nothing, but too much, *all*, remains
of her to be given.
"I wish I could love a little girl like you." Just
as a woman says to a man: "I wish I could love
a little you." Again you. Again a you. A you,
birthed by me.

Finally, it is the desperate cry, raw, incurable:
"A child of yours!"

¶

The one who will never come. The one whose coming you cannot even implore. You can ask the Virgin for a child of the male lover, you can ask the Virgin for a child of an old man—an injustice—a miracle—but you do not ask for something mad. A union from which the child is simply excluded. A state of affairs involving the absence of the child. Unthinkable. Everything but a child. As at that dinner with the great king and the nobleman: everything but the bread. The daily bread—of women.

¶

It is the desperate desire of only one of them, the younger one, the one most *she*. The older one, she does not need a child, she can be a mother to her love. "You are my love, you are my god, you are my all."

But the other doesn't want to be loved like a child, she wants a child to love.

And so she who began by not wanting a child of *his*, will end up wanting a child of *hers*. And because this cannot be, she will leave one day, still in love, but hounded by the lucid and powerless jealousy of the other—and on another day she will wash ashore, a ruin, in the arms of the first man to come along.

⁋

(My child, my love, my all, and—your brilliant phrase, Madame—"*mon frère féminin*," never; sister. It seems that the word sister scares these women, as if it could reintegrate them by force into a world they had turned away from forever.)

In the beginning, the older one fears it more than the younger one desires it. One could even say that the older one creates the younger's despair, turning a smile into a sigh, a sigh into desire, desire into obsession. The obsession of the older one leads to the obsession of the younger. "You will leave, you will leave, you will leave. You want it from me, you will want it from the first man to come... it is again of this that you are thinking... you looked at that man. Aren't you thinking—what a father for your child! Go away, then, since I cannot give it to you."

⁋

Our apprehensions evoke, our fears suggest,

our obsessions incarnate. The younger one, after being silent for so long, thinks of it constantly, she only has eyes for the young women with full arms. And to think that I will never have one, since I will never, never leave her. (It is in this moment that she leaves her.)

¶

The child—a fixed point from which, henceforth, she will not remove her eyes. The repressed child surfaces in her eyes like one drowned. You would have to be blind not to see him there.

And the one that began by wanting a child of *hers* will end up wanting a child of anyone, even of him she loathes. The persecuting him becomes the savior. The lover—she is the enemy. In this way the wind returns in its circles.

¶

The child begins in us long before his beginning. There are some pregnancies that last for years of hope, for eternities of despair.

¶

And all those friends who get married. And the

husbands of those friends, so light-hearted, so open, so very close… And to think that I also could have…

Walled up.

Buried alive.

¶

And the other works at it. Innuendos, suspicions, criticisms.

The younger: "You do not love me anymore?"

"I love you, but—well, since you will leave."

You will leave, you will leave, you will leave.

¶

Before leaving she will want to die. Then, in the middle of death, without knowing, without deliberating beforehand, without thinking, by pure and triple vital instinct—youth, perpetuation, womb—she will hear herself laughing and joking at the hour of the never-missed meeting on the other side of town—and of life—with anyone—the husband of one of her friends or the subordinate of her father, as long as it is not *her*.

Man, after woman, how simple and kind. How straightforward. How free! How pure.

¶

Then, the end will come. The beginning of the male lover? The succession of male lovers? The stability of the husband?

The child will come.

¶

I omit the exceptional case: the non-maternal woman.

I also omit the banal case: the young woman who is depraved, either out of instinct or fashion, the shallow pleasure-lover.

I omit, as well, the lost soul, the unusual case of one who in love searches for soul, thus—predestined to choose a woman.

And the one who loves with abandon, who, in matters of love, searches for love and takes it where she will.

And the medical case.

I consider the normal case, the natural and vital

case of a young woman who is wary of man and drawn toward woman and wants a child. She who, between the man (the stranger, the indifferent, or even the *revealing* enemy) and the *repressive* beloved, ends up choosing the enemy.

She who prefers having a child to love.

She who prefers her child to her love.

¶

Because the child is innate, he is in us before love, before the lover. His desire to exist causes us to open our arms. A young girl—I speak of those from the North—is always too young for love, never for the child. When she is thirteen—she dreams of him.

Something innate that must be given to us. Some begin by loving the giver, others end up loving him, or end up submitting to him, or not submitting to him anymore.

Something innate that must be given to us. The one who doesn't give it to us takes it from us.

¶

Ungrateful like all who love no more, unjust

like those who still do, we will find her again, with full arms and a heart full of hate for the one she will henceforth describe as an error of youth.

§

She will not be caught that way again.

§

Don't hold it against me. I am responding to the Amazon, not to the fair feminine vision who asks nothing of me. Not to the one who gave me the book, but to the one who wrote it.

If you had not mentioned the child, I would have recognized a deliberate omission, in silence a final renunciation, a scar that I would have respected. But you come back to it, you throw it like a ball: "What gives women the right to make and unmake life? Two children— two careless mistakes?" etc.

§

It is the only weak point, the only assailable point, the only breach in the perfect entity of two women who love one another. The impossible is not to resist the temptation of a man, but the need for a child.

¶

This single weak point ruins the whole cause. This single assailable point allows the entire enemy body to enter. Because even if we could one day have a child *without him*, we could never have a child of hers, a little you to love.

¶

(An adopted daughter? Neither yours, nor mine? With, in addition, two mothers? How well nature makes that which she makes.)

The child: the only assailable point, which ruins the whole cause. The only point that saves the cause of man. And of humanity.

¶

An entity too whole. A unity too one. ("Two shall be one." No—two shall be *three*.) A road that leads nowhere. An impasse. Let's retrace our steps.

¶

However beautiful you are, however much you are *the one*—the first boor to come along will triumph over you. He will be blessed. While you will remain damned.

¶

"But it is the same as not being able to have a child with the male lover. Would that be a reason to leave him?"

An exceptional case cannot be compared to a law without exception. The entire race, the entire cause, the entire matter is sentenced when women love one another.

To leave an infertile man for his fertile brother is different from leaving the eternally-barren love for the eternally-fertile enemy. In the former case, I bid farewell to a man; in the latter, to the entire race, the entire cause, to all women in a single one.

To change only the object. To change shores and worlds.

Oh! I know, sometimes it lasts until death—the touching and terrifying vision of two old women on a wild bank in Crimea, having spent their lives together. One of them was the sister of the great Slavic thinker, so read nowadays in France. Same luminous forehead, same stormy eyes, and same fleshy bare lips. But the emptiness around them was more empty than the emptiness that surrounds the "usual" old and infertile couple, a vacuum more isolating, more draining.

Only, only because of that—damned race.

❡

If the younger one is not shallow, the horror of this curse may be what makes her leave.

"What people say" does not have weight, must not have weight, since what is said is ill-spoken, what is seen, ill-seen. The evil eye of envy, of curiosity, of indifference. The world, wallowing in evil, has nothing to say.

God? Once and for all, God has nothing to do with sensual love. His name, joined or opposed to any other loved name, be it masculine or feminine, rings of sacrilege. Christ and sensual love are incommensurable. God has nothing to do with our woes, except to cure us of them. He said once and for all: "Love me, the Eternal." Apart from this—all is vain. Equally, irremediably vain. By simply loving another with that sensual love, I betray the One who died on the cross of the other love for me and for my neighbor.

The Church and the State? No fault can be found

as long as thousands of young men are driven to kill each other and are blessed for doing so.

But what will, what does, nature—the sole avenger and legislator of our physical deviations—say? Nature says: no. In forbidding it to us, she protects herself. God, in forbidding us something, does so out of love; nature, in forbidding us, does so out of love for herself, out of hate for all that is not her. Nature hates the cloister as much as the island where the head of Orpheus landed. Her vengeance is our ruin. Only, in the cloister, God is there to help us; while on the island, there is only the sea in which to drown ourselves.

§

The island—earth which is not, from which you cannot depart, that you must love because you are condemned to it. A place from which you see everything, from which you can do nothing.

Earth upon which one can count one's steps. Impasse.

The great poet, that great sorrowful soul, chose well the place of her birth.

¶

Brotherhood of lepers.

¶

Outside of nature. But how is it then that the young girl, a being of nature, is so completely, so trustingly, misled?

This is a snare of the soul. By falling into the arms of the older, she is caught in neither the trap of nature, nor in that of the beloved, who is too often seen as a sorceress, a huntress, a bird of prey, even—a vampire, when she is, nearly always, a severe and noble being whose only crime is to foresee what will come and, let us say it now, to see the lover go. The young girl is caught in the snare of the soul.

She wants to love—but… she would like it— if… and there she is in the arms of the other, her head against the elder's chest, where the *soul* resides.

Push her away? Try asking that of a man, old or young.

¶

Then, the encounter. Unexpected and inevitable since—though you live henceforth in different worlds—the earth is yet one: the one where you walk.

Shock of heart, ebb and flow of blood. Woman's first and last weapon—with which she disarms, believes she disarms even death— her weary bravado—living blade and suddenly red—the smile. Next, the small incoherent rush of syllables tumbling one over the other, like small folds of water over stones. What did she say? Nothing, since the other heard nothing, as we never hear the first words. But the other, having taken her eyes from the animated mouth, now detects that this movement has a meaning: ...ten months... a dear... he prefers me to all... he weighs... (Swallow, swallow, swallow more, choke it down—for everything you did to me!)... As I was saying—he weighs... (more than the entire earth, more than the whole sea on the heart of the older).

The fullness of revenge! And in the younger's eyes—what hatred! The hatred of a slave who has at last been freed. The sweetness of putting your foot on a heart.

And the little torrent damned for good—undulations slow and lilting, crystalline: "Would you like to come to see me, to see us, my husband and me?"

¶

She has forgotten nothing. She remembers too well.

¶

Then comes the bath, a daily ritual, sacrosanct. Evident—and nearly indecent—triumph of virility. For it is inevitably a son, always a son, as if nature, impatient to make her rights known, was loath to linger on the detour of a girl. Not the little you, implored and impossible—the little him, uncomplicated, unrequested, custom-built, mere result (the great purpose!).

The other, hanging on to her last hope, or simply at a loss for words:

"He looks like you."

"No" (sharp and clear).

And the last sting, which perhaps extinguishes the remnants of this great poison that is love:

"He looks like his father. He is the living image of my husband."

There is intentional vulgarity in this vindictiveness. She uses only the words she knows to be the most hurtful, the most common, the words everyone uses (look at the everyday type that you loved!). Choice or instinct? It comes to her without thought, she hears herself speak (as on that day, already distant, when she heard herself laugh). Then, the ritual ended, Moses saved and clothed, she puts him to her breast and— supreme vindictiveness—peers through her lowered lashes for the flash of desire drowned in a blur of tenderness in the eyes of the elder. For there is in the depths of any woman, if she is not a monster, for there is even in the depths of all monsters... for there are no monsters among women.

That flash, that smile—she is *aware* of them, but—for one reason or another—she will not lift her eyes.

If the man is intelligent, he will never ask of her: "What are you thinking about?"

Perhaps, once the other is gone, she will want to beat her head against a wall.

Perhaps, once the other is gone, she will not want to offer her lips.

If the man is intelligent, he will not kiss her immediately, he will wait—to kiss—until the other is gone—forever.

¶

(Why did she come? To hurt herself. It is, sometimes, all that we have left.)

¶

Then, there will be the other encounter, the second encounter, then there will be *retribution*.

Same earth (outside of this, nothing is worth mentioning, since everything that takes place takes place inside).

Same spectators watching and listening. (The last vengeful act of nature: for having been too alone, too one, too much everything for each other, henceforth when they meet everyone and everything will be between them.)

Same time: the eternity of youth, while it *is*.

"Look, isn't that your friend passing?"

"Where?"

"There, with the brunette dressed in blue."

Before having seen, she knows.

And here it is that the human tide more inhuman and ineluctable than that of the sea, brings to her, brings her to…

This time, the older begins: "How are you?" (and without waiting, without hearing): "Allow me to introduce my friend, Mademoiselle such-and-such." (A name.)

If the former lover, who has grown pale under her powder, "was" fair—then the new one, the replacement, without fail, will be dark. If made entirely of grace—made entirely of strength. Posthumous faithfulness? Desire for a complete death? Or a last strike to the memories? A grudge toward all blondeness? To kill blonde with brown? It is a law. Ask men why.

Some looks kill. But no looks are exchanged, since the brunette leaves, very much alive on the arm of the older one—the loved one. The blue waves of the new lover's long dress envelop her, placing between the one who stays and the one who leaves the impossibility of the sea.

⁋

That night, leaning over the adored sleeper: Ah! Jean, if you knew, if you knew, if you knew…

It is not on the day when the child is born but today, three years later, that she knows how much he has cost her.

⁋

As long as the other is young, she will always be seen accompanied by a living shadow.

The brunette will change: will become blonde again or red-headed. The brunette will leave as the blonde left. As all who walk toward an unknown destination—always the same—must leave, having rested a while under the tree that remains.

⁋

They all will pass. All would pass through her arms if… But we do not stay eternally young.

⁋

The other! Let's think of her. The island. The eternally isolated. The mother losing all of her daughters one by one, losing them for eternity, for not only will they never come to place their children in her arms, but, also, catching a glimpse of her at the turn of a street, they will furtively make the sign of a cross on the head of their little ones. Niobe, with her feminine line of descent, destroyed by a fiercer hunter. Eternally losing the only game that matters—the only game there is. The loathed. The banished. The damned. White bodiless vision whose race we recognize only by the knowing, recognizing, appraising gaze in which the auctioneer is joined to the idolater, the chess player to the beatified—a gaze with multiple layers in which the last is always the last but one, endless, bottomless (all qualifiers will be consumed, because it is a chasm)—ineffable gaze, effaced by the wintry smile of renouncement.

When they are young women, you recognize them by their smile. Old, it is by their smile that you mistake them.

Young or old, it is they who look the most soulful. All the other women with the look of flesh *are not it*, do not belong, or are it only for a short while.

She lives on an island. She creates an island. She

is an island. Island, with its boundless community of souls. Who knows if in that moment, in the Indies, there, at the edge of the world… A young girl, tying back her brown hair…

Uncertainties—they sustain us.

And that remains the most sure.

¶

The older one will die alone, because she is too proud to love a dog, remembers too well to adopt a child. She does not want animals, nor orphans, not a lady's companion, old or young. King David, warming himself by the dull heat of Abishag, was a lout. She does not want bought warmth, nor a ready smile. She wants to be neither vampire nor grandmother. That is fine for the men who, old, content themselves with scraps, with living alongside other sides, with rubbing shoulders, with smiles intended for other mouths—intercepted smiles, stolen at random. "Pass by, little girls, pass by…" She will never be the poor relation at the feast of another's youth. Neither friendship, nor respect, nor this other abyss that is our own kindness. She will put nothing in the place of love. She will not give up the splendid darkness, the black and round burn—a circle more magical than yours, Faust!—of the bonfire of yesteryear. Each coming spring—she will hold firm.

Even if a young woman throws herself against her as a child throws itself against a passerby or against a wall—passerby, she will avoid; wall, she will be immutable. Pride will make this once ardent lover pure. She who all her life was fearsome will no longer want to be fearsome in this way. The young demon will never become the old lamia.

Kindness—haughtiness—distance.

"Pass quickly, girls mad and beautiful."

§

Under the walls of a powder store
Nearly overthrown by time
Hand in front of your splendor
Pass by, young girls, pass by.

And as for him—it is in the rightful glory of all their blondeness past that he passes. She—in a condensation of horror.

Over her fatal and natural inclination, neither

God, nor man, nor her own pity had any power, but her pride will. And her pride alone. And so well that the forever young, quite intimidated, says to her mother: "That lady frightens me. She looks so hard. Have I displeased her?"

And another, brought to "the lady" by her mother—who knows why?—hears said to her in a voice imperceptibly cracked by repression: "Your mother told me you have a disposition for painting. You must cultivate your talents, Mademoiselle…"

Never painted, never tinted, never made younger, enhanced, altered, leaving all of that to "normal" older women, those who before everyone's eyes, and with the blessing of the priest, wed at sixty in righteous union with a child of twenty. She leaves that to the sisters of Caesar.

¶

A fatal and natural tendency of the mountain for the valley, the torrent for the lake.

Toward evening, the mountain flows back completely toward its peak. When night comes, it is peak. It seems that its torrents are flowing backwards. At night, she pulls herself together.

¶

...Then, another day, the one who was young will learn that somewhere, on the other side of the earth, the older one died. First she will want to write to know more. But time, hurrying by—the letter will come to a halt. The desire will remain desire. The *I must know* will become *I wish*; then—*I no longer wish*. "To what end, since she is already dead? Since I too will die one day..." And bravely, with the great honesty of indifference: "Since she died in me—for me—a good twenty years ago?"

To be dead there is no need to die.

¶

Island. Peak. Alone.

¶

Weeping willow! Mournful willow! Willow, body and soul of women! Mournful nape of the neck of the willow. Gray hair in front of the face, so that nothing more is seen. Gray hair sweeping the face of the earth.

The waters, the air, the mountains, the trees are given to us to understand the human soul, so profoundly hidden. When I see a willow in despair I understand Sappho.

Clamart, Nov.-Dec. 1932.

(copied and revised in November 1934, with a little more gray hair. MT).